The Potoma Family

PIONEERS OF PHOTOGRAPHY

PIONEERS OF PHOTOGRAPHY

EVA WEBER

SMITHMARK

This edition published in 1995
by SMITHMARK Publishers Inc.,
16 East 32nd Street
New York, New York 10016.

SMITHMARK books are available for bulk purchase
for sales promotion and premium use. For details
write or telephone the Manager of Special Sales,
SMITHMARK Publishers Inc., 16 East 32nd Street,
New York, NY 10016. (212) 532-6600.

Produced by Brompton Books Corp.,
15 Sherwood Place,
Greenwich, CT 06830

ISBN 0-8317-1030-6

Printed in Spain

10 9 8 7 6 5 4 3 2 1

Page 1
TONI FRISSELL
MIDSUMMER NIGHT'S DREAM, 1947
LIBRARY OF CONGRESS, WASHINGTON, DC

Page 2
GERTRUDE KÄSEBIER
HAPPY DAYS, 1902
Gum bichromate print, $12\frac{5}{8} \times 10$ in.
LIBRARY OF CONGRESS, WASHINGTON, DC

Page 5
GUSTAVE LE GRAY
SEA AND SKY, 1856
VICTORIA & ALBERT MUSEUM, LONDON

CONTENTS

INTRODUCTION

The "mirror with the memory," the "shadow catcher," and the "pencil of nature" were some of the poetic phrases used to describe photography upon its discovery. To nineteenth-century enthusiasts of this new art, the making of a photograph, which fixed forever a moment of time, resembled an act of magic. This magic, indescribable in familiar terms, required a new metaphoric vocabulary. Hence the early name of heliography (or writing by the sun) was recast as photography (or writing by light) when improved equipment and processes allowed the camera to move indoors into the studio. Yet the romantic attitude toward photography persisted, as seen in an 1859 article in *The Atlantic Monthly* by Oliver Wendell Holmes, eminent Boston physician, essayist and amateur photographer. In an attempt to explain photography to the lay public in non-technical terms, he proposed a vivid analogy based on theories from ancient philosophy: each time a picture was taken by the camera, a membrane or microscopically thin layer of surface matter was cast off by the subject. This film was then permanently fixed on paper, metal or glass by means of the alchemy of chemistry.

Well before 1839, the official date of photography's birth, the camera, as we know it, had been developed as an aid to drawing. As early as the fifth century B.C. the Chinese had noted that light rays passing through a pinhole in a wall into a dark chamber would cast an exact but upside-down version of the scene outside onto the inside wall facing the pinhole. This optical phenomenon was recorded by successive generations of observers, notably Aristotle in fourth century B.C. Greece, Arab scholar Ibn-Al-Haitham in the tenth century A.D., and by European scientists beginning with Roger Bacon in the thirteenth century. Writings from around 1560 indicate that the camera obscura (literally "dark room") was in use by artists, and soon a portable version was constructed, consisting of a long closed box with a lens at one end that could focus an image of the scene before the lens onto an angled mirror at the other end. The mirror then reflected the image up onto a translucent piece of glass set into the top of the box. The artist placed a thin sheet of paper on this glass and traced the reflected image. The next stage lay in finding a way to fix, or permanently preserve the camera image.

The chemistry of photography began to develop in the seventeenth century with the identification of such light-sensitive compounds as silver nitrate and silver chloride. The 1725 discovery by Johann Heinrich Schulze that sunlight caused silver nitrate to darken inspired further studies of the effects of light on various chemical salts. Beginning in 1799, Thomas Wedgwood, son of the famous English pottery manufacturer Josiah Wedgwood, was the first to use these results, with the help of chemist Humphry Davy. They placed objects such as tree leaves and insect wings, and later miniature paintings on glass, on top of paper and white leather treated with a silver nitrate solution and then exposed them to sunlight. According to Davy's 1802 report on their work, they initially were successful in producing a negative image (a white silhouette on a dark background), but were unable to stop the action of light on the silver nitrate. Unless the picture was then kept in the dark, the image subsequently vanished.

The first photographic image inside the camera obscura was made in France in 1816 by Joseph Nicéphore Niépce (1765-1833) and his brother Claude. Niépce used paper moistened with a silver chloride solution, but was unable to make positive prints from the unstable negative image. He then tried using a glass plate coated with bitumen to copy engravings on oiled paper (to make them translucent) and exposing them to sunlight to make contact prints. This heliography, as he called it, was intended to make etched plates from which inked prints could be reproduced in large quantities. Finally he turned to coating metal plates with bitumen, and in 1827 successfully produced a camera obscura view of his courtyard on a bitumen-coated pewter plate—the first permanent photograph in history.

Following a disappointing five-month trip to England in 1827 on which he failed to find support because he refused to disclose the details of his process, Niépce eventually agreed to collaborate with Louis Jacques Mandé Daguerre (1787-1851), a successful Parisian theater designer and painter of the popular spectacle known as the diorama. Daguerre's use of the

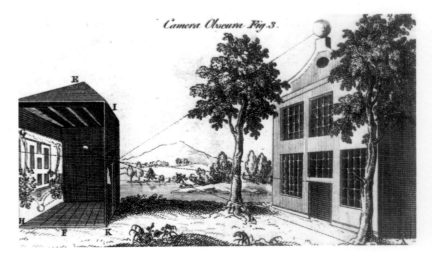

Right: The earliest surviving photograph taken in 1827 by Nicéphore Niépce. He produced this view from his studio window on pewter plate coated with bitumen.

Bottom right: A plaster bust of Nicéphore Niépce made by Jean August Barre in 1853.

Opposite bottom: An eighteenth-century engraving of a camera obscura. Note the inverted image of the house on the wall opposite the opening.

camera obscura to make preliminary studies for diorama scenes led him to begin experimenting with ways to fix the camera image in the early 1820s. Daguerre and Niépce both ordered lenses from the same optician and by this means, Daguerre had learned of Niépce's secretive work. Daguerre first wrote to Niépce in 1825, Niépce visited him in Paris in 1827, and finally in 1829 they formally initiated a partnership to share the results of their individual research and to perfect a camera image process.

After Niépce's death in 1833, Daguerre found a way to sensitize a silver-coated copper plate with iodine fumes and to produce a direct positive image without the use of Niépce's bitumen coating. A crucial success came in 1835 when he discovered the phenomenon of the latent image: the camera image does not appear during the exposure of the plate, but is revealed later only during the chemical development process. At the same time, he found a way to bring out this latent image by using mercury vapor, considerably shortening the required exposure time. The fixing process – making the image permanent – was the final hurdle Daguerre surmounted in 1837 by washing the exposed and developed plate with a solution of salt water. In March 1839 he changed the fixing solution to hyposulphite of soda, a method discovered in 1819 by English scientist Sir John Herschel (1792-1871).

Although Daguerre's discovery was not announced until January 7, 1839, he offered Niépce's heliographic method and his own daguerreotype process for sale at a very high price in 1838. When this failed, he turned to the French government which in 1839 purchased both inventions outright and in effect presented them to the world, probably because the copyrights would have

been impossible to enforce. On August 19, 1839 a crowded meeting of scientists and others observed Daguerre's demonstration of his process. His sensational discovery was then rapidly reported worldwide. For a while, Daguerre demonstrated his process to various other groups and arranged for the production of instruction manuals and cameras, but he gradually withdrew from the fray. Others were to make the next significant advances in photography.

While his discovery may have been the first to be announced publicly, Daguerre was not the only one at work on the possibilities of photography. As was the case with many other important discoveries, photography was an idea whose time had come. In 1834, William Henry Fox Talbot (1800-1877), an English country gentleman scholar and scientist, began trying to fix a camera obscura image on paper. By 1835 he was making exquisite "photogenic drawings," as he called them, or contact prints, by placing botanical specimens and pieces of lace on sheets of good quality writing paper sensitized with silver chloride and silver nitrate, exposing them to sunlight, and then fixing them with a

rinse of hot salt water. (Like Daguerre, he also changed his fixative to hyposulphite of soda in 1839 on Herschel's recommendation). He also made a small negative image of his home, Lacock Abbey, on sensitized paper in 1835. Temporarily losing interest in photography he turned his attention to other studies. When news of Daguerre's discovery reached him, he went back to experimenting, independently discovering the latent image and its development in 1840, as well as the process of making multiple positive paper prints from a single paper negative. He worked hard to perfect his paper process and patented it in February 1841 as the calotype (from the Greek, meaning beautiful image), also known as the talbotype.

Top: The earliest extant photograph on glass, taken in September 1839 by Sir John Herschel of a scaffolding.

Left: William Henry Fox Talbot's camera obscura.

Opposite: An 1844 daguerreotype taken by Jean Baptiste Sabatier-Blot of Louis Jacques Mande Daguerre.

In the early years of photography, the calotype could not begin to match the popularity of the daguerreotype with its sharp detail, lustrous surface and tonal richness. As no negative was involved in the process, each daguerreotype was a unique image, elegantly set into a velvet-lined ornamental case in order to protect its fragile surface. By comparison, the detail in the calotype was much softer and the picture was often mottled from the paper fibers that lay beneath. Undoubtedly Talbot himself was the most effective deterrent to the spread of the calotype. Enforcing his patent on the process, he prosecuted anyone using it without first procuring an expensive license. At the same time, Talbot sought popular acceptance for the calotype by setting up a small factory in 1843 to mass produce high quality photographic prints and to publish *The Pencil of Nature* in 1844. This book, the first to be illustrated with photographs, included Talbot's views of Paris and Oxford, and of sculpture and drawings. However, the calotype salt prints tipped into the book tended to fade eventually, which also worked against the acceptance of Talbot's process. Despite all this, Talbot, in contrast to Daguerre, remained active in the photographic scene, continuing to experiment, to improve processes and to make some 600 photographs during the rest of

his career. His most significant discovery, the reproducible negative, came to be applied universally only with the development of the wet-plate collodion process in 1851.

Others, as well, shared in the discovery of photography. In 1833 Antoine Hercules Florence, a French artist in Brazil, started to experiment with producing direct positive paper prints of drawings. Most importantly, Hippolyte Bayard (1801-1887), a French civil servant in the Ministry of Finance, began experimenting in 1837 and by 1839 had created a method for making direct positive prints on paper. Official support for the daguerreotype overshadowed Bayard's achievement. Discouraged but persistent, he went on to work with the calotype and other photographic processes. As a photographer he produced a large body of high quality work, covering a wide range of subject matter from still lifes, portraits, cityscapes, and architectural views to a record of the barricades of the 1848 revolution. Other pioneers include Joseph Bancroft Reade, an English clergyman, and Hans Thøger Winther, a Norwegian publisher and attorney.

Less dramatic discoveries, some minor but others far-reaching, continued to refine the photographic process throughout the nineteenth century. In 1851

Above: A calotype (or talbotype) of the Reading Photographic Establishment taken in 1844 by William Henry Fox Talbot.

Gustave Le Gray (1820-1882) announced his development of a waxed-paper negative process. While other photographers sometimes waxed their paper negatives for greater translucency after developing them, Le Gray waxed the paper before exposure, resulting in a smoother surface and sharper detail in the image. The possibility of preparing the negative in advance appealed to traveling photographers, some of whom preferred Le Gray's method over the collodion glass negative process. A leading figure in French photography, Le Gray was a former painter who became an accomplished photographer of seascapes, landscapes, architectural views and military life. He also became an influential teacher of Maxime Du Camp, Charles Nègre and Henri Le Secq among others and wrote a number of instruction manuals on photographic technique.

In 1848 English sculptor Frederick Scott Archer (1813-1857) invented the wet-plate collodion process which was to revolutionize photography by replacing the daguerreotype and calotype processes, beginning around 1855. Collodion was a syrupy mixture of gun cotton dissolved in alcohol and ether, with potassium iodide added. Coated with this solution, glass-plate negatives were then chemically sensitized and exposed while still wet. The plate had to be developed immediately afterward, in a dark tent or wagon if the photographer was out in the field. After a protective coat of varnish was applied, the developed glass-plate negative could be taken back to the studio to make prints. The collodion process was highly regarded because in very short exposure times, it produced images with great clarity of detail and range of tone.

Although the salt paper print invented by Talbot (1840s-1850s) and the albumen paper print (1850s-1890s) became the standard for nineteenth-century photographers, a variety of print types emerged. In 1842 Sir John Herschel invented the cyanotype process. Using iron salts to sensitize the paper, he obtained a blue-tinted image. The blueprint method of duplicating architectural drawings was later derived from this process, as well as the kallitype process (1899) which could produce prints in tones of black, brown, sepia, purple or maroon. The carbon print, developed in the late 1850s, remained in use from the mid-1860s through 1910. In this process gelatin combined with potassium bichromate and carbon black or another pigment coated lightweight paper and yielded prints valued for their permanence, rich glossy black or brown tones, or other tints, depending on the pigment.

In the gelatin silver print, also known as the silver-bromide print or the silver-chloride print, introduced in the early 1870s, gelatin emulsion permeated with silver salts coated paper to produce a range of tones and surface gloss. Commercially available after the 1880s, gelatin silver print papers generally replaced albumen paper by the mid-1890s, because of their relative ease of production and because of their greater stability – they did not yellow over time as did albumen prints. The platinum print (or platinotype) and its successor, the palladium print (or palladiotype) were appreciated especially by artistic photographers until the 1920s for their subtle tonalities ranging from exquisite silvery grays through rose-browns. Depending on a modulation of temperature, developing compounds or post-development rinses, hues of reds, blues or olive greens could be obtained. The platinum process was patented in England in 1873 by William Willis (1841-1923), who began commercial production of platinum paper in 1878.

Pictorialist photographers also valued the gum-bichromate process which allowed great artistic latitude in choice of pigment, paper, variations in development and other manipulations. An offshoot of the gum-bichromate process was the bromoil or oil pigment print (1907-1930s) which employed greasy lithographic inks and a transfer process to produce prints of a variety of hues, or by applying a number of different colors to produce a full range of added colors on a single print. Color photography was not developed until 1904 when Louis Lumière (1864-1948) patented the autochrome, the first practical color process. The color in nineteenth-century photographs had been added after exposure, either during development by varying chemical compounds or by adding pigment, or on the photographic print by hand tinting.

Archer's collodion process led to the invention of several new subspecies of photographic image. One was the ambrotype, also created by Archer, but named after James Ambrose Cutting (1814-1867), a Philadelphia photographer who patented a way of encasing the negative collodion image on glass which, when placed over a dark backing, appeared as a positive image. Like daguerreotypes, ambrotypes were unique images and were presented similarly in elaborate hinged cases. Because of the relative ease of their production and their low cost, ambrotypes replaced the daguerreotypes as a popular portrait medium by the later 1850s.

The tintype, or the ferrotype, also followed the collodion process. A thin iron sheet coated with a black or brown lacquer was then covered with collodion, sensitized and exposed in the camera. A camera with twelve or sixteen lenses could yield a sheet of postage-stamp-size tintypes to be cut apart after development. Larger sizes were also available. Frequently offered by street vendors, the inexpensive tintype remained popular until the turn of the century, making portrait photography accessible to the masses.

During the collodion era, from about 1855 to 1881, the mass production of photographs from the wet-plate glass negative became an economically feasible venture. The widest publication and distribution of photographs came in the form of cartes-de-visite, and numbered series of stereographs and album cards featuring specific themes, places or events. The carte-de-visite was introduced in France in 1854 by studio photographer André-Adolphe Eugène Disdéri (1819-1889) when he patented a way to divide a collodion glass-plate negative into ten smaller negative areas, thus allowing the exposure of ten separate poses on the

BRADY'S DAGUERREOTYPES

WERE AWARDED / THE

WORLD'S FAIR, IN LONDON,

1851,

THE PRIZE MEDAL,

For the Best Daguerreotypes in New York.

BRADY'S DAGUERREOTYPES have invariably commanded the highest prizes whenever offered for competition.

The proprietor has no hesitation in claiming for his new Gallery, 359 Broadway, advantages possessed by no similar establishment either in this country or in Europe. The facilities for the production of

First Class Pictures,

are unrivaled. An additional building has been erected, by which the Reception Saloon, Ladies' Dressing Room, and Operating Rooms are on the same floor, thus forming a new and most desirable arrangement.

This Gallery, in connection with the Old Establishment, 205 Broadway, corner of Fulton Street, contains a collection of American and European celebrities unrivaled on this continent.

single plate. These 3½ inch by 2¼ inch images, which were often portraits of celebrities or scenic views, were glued to stiff paper mounts the size of formal visiting cards. Produced by the millions, cartes-de-visite often were collected into albums. The somewhat larger (about 6 inch by 4 inch) cabinet card photo, introduced in the 1860s, also sold well. By the 1890s, mass-produced scenic postcards eclipsed both versions of the card photograph.

The stereograph, also introduced in the 1850s, had a much longer life, remaining popular through the middle of the twentieth century. A three-dimensional illusion was produced when two separate views of the same subject taken from twin lenses about the same distance apart as the human eyes were examined through special viewers. The multiple prints from

Above: Stereograph pictures mounted on cards were viewed with a stereoscope which produced a three-dimensional illusion.

Right: The popular cartes-de-visite were used as photographic calling cards. This example is of Dr. Mary Walker, the first woman awarded the Medal of Honor in the United States.

Opposite: An advertisement for Mathew Brady's gallery of celebrities and daguerreotype services citing the prize medal he won at the World's Fair in 1851.

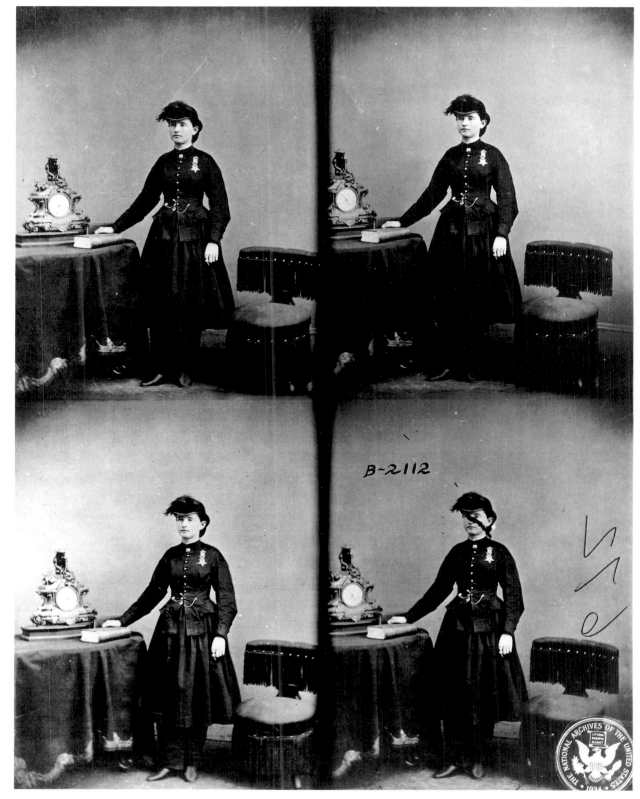

twin- or triple-lensed cameras could also be cut apart to be sold as individual cartes-de-visite.

A special viewing device also was required for the photographic lantern slide. Before the 1850s, magic lanterns, as the primitive projectors were known, had been used to cast images of paintings on glass onto walls or screens. Like stereographs, magic lantern slides became a popular home entertainment, or were used by public lecturers, some of whom were noted photographers discussing and displaying their work.

The development of albumen print paper accompanied the collodion revolution. In 1850, Louis-Désiré Blanquart-Evrard (1802-1872) invented the albumen paper print which was to remain the standard until the 1890s. Albumen paper, prepared by first coating it with a layer of egg white, provided a glossy surface and a clarity of detail far surpassing the performance of the salt print. Blanquart-Evrard established the first commercial photofinishing and photographic publishing house, Imprimerie Photographie, in 1851. He published many photographic books and albums, including Maxime Du Camp's views of Egypt, Nubia, Palestine and Syria (1852), John B. Greene's series on the Nile (1854), and Auguste Salzmann's Jerusalem images (1856). With his assembly-line production system Blanquart-Evrard had hoped to reduce the cost of fine photographs to around five centimes, but this turned out to be a serious miscalculation. The sale price of his prints ended up much higher than that of the popular lithographs, the ubiquitous visual mass medium of nineteenth-century Europe and America.

The sale and distribution of photographic images through a variety of outlets was key to the acceptance of photography as a documentary and artistic medium far surpassing the graphic arts and painting in immediacy and realism. Pioneering ventures such as Blanquart-Evrard's and Talbot's publishing firms met with mixed success. Francis Frith (1822-1898) made his own views taken on expeditions to Egypt and the Middle East the foundation of the largest English photographic print and publishing house, which was to remain active until 1968. Frith hired other cameramen to take views of America, Europe and Great Britain, and he purchased Roger Fenton's negatives, as well as the work of other photographers.

Most profitable were the large numbers of stereographs sold by the London Stereoscopic and Photographic Company, Loescher and Petsch in Germany, Gaudin in France, and the E. and H. T. Anthony Company in the United States. Edward Anthony (1819-1888) started out in the 1840s as a daguerreotypist who photographed all the important members of government in his Washington studio. In 1847 in New York he established, with his brother, what was to become the largest American photographic supply house. The Anthonys soon expanded to publish the nation's leading photographic journal, as well as cartes-de-visite and stereographs from purchased and commissioned negatives. Their extension of credit in the form of supplies and equipment made possible Mathew Brady's historic coverage of the Civil War.

Brady (1823-1896) made his mark as a celebrated portrait photographer in the 1840s and 1850s, opening studios in New York and Washington, but he was somewhat less successful as a publisher. His *Gallery of Illustrious Americans* (1850), containing twelve lithographs based on Brady studio portraits, did not sell well. Nor did his attempt to pay for his Civil War expenses with the sale of stereographs of the conflict succeed. Although the era's leading pictorial journals, such as *Harper's Weekly*, reported on the Civil War extensively, they had to rely on engraved and not always accurate versions of the battlefield made by Brady's cameramen and other photographers. Nineteenth-century photomechanical methods of reproduction – photolithography, the collotype, the Woodburytype and photogravure – yielded high quality images, but the direct printing of photographs on newspaper or periodical pages was not possible until the introduction of the halftone process in the 1890s.

Throughout the nineteenth century, each refinement of the photographic process led to a new flourishing of talented photographers, sometimes in a single region or nation, and at other times globally. It is generally agreed that during the daguerreotype era an exceptionally fine body of work came from the United States. In March 1839 Daguerre personally demonstrated his process to inventor and painter Samuel Morse (1791-1872) who enthusiastically returned to New York to open a studio with John Draper (1811-1882), a British-born professor and doctor. Draper took the first photograph of the moon in March 1840 (a feat

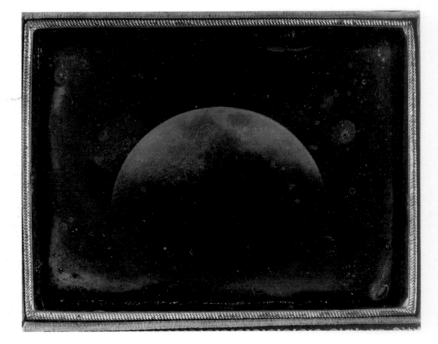

Right: Mathew Brady, who became one of the most important Civil War photographers in America, shown immediately after his return from the first battle of Bull Run in 1861.

Opposite: One of the best early daguerreotypes of the moon in existence, taken by J. A. Whipple at the 15-inch refractor of the Harvard College Observatory in Cambridge, Massachusetts, on February 26, 1852.

Photo taken July 22ⁿᵈ 1861

BRADY The Photographer returned from Bull Run

to be repeated by Boston's John Adams Whipple in 1852), as well as the earliest surviving portrait, of his sister Dorothy Catherine Draper. Morse taught the daguerreotype process to Edward Anthony, Albert Southworth and possibly Mathew Brady, all of whom became leading daguerreotypists.

Engraver Joseph Saxton's very early view of a Phil-

adelphia school was eclipsed by the subsequent finely detailed architectural images of Washington government buildings by John Plumbe (1809-1857), who operated a chain of fourteen studios from Boston to New Orleans during the 1840s. The daguerreotype was most in demand for portraits, which had previously been available only in the form of paintings,

silhouettes, and profile drawings made by Saint-Memin's physionotrace. One of the most highly regarded portrait studios was that of the Boston partners Albert Sands Southworth (1811-1894) and Josiah Johnson Hawes (1808-1901). Philadelphia's Langenheim brothers, Friedrich (1809-1879) and Wilhelm (1807-1874), made a comfortable career of portraiture but sought fame with a five-plate panorama of Niagara Falls (1845). A view of the July 5, 1853 Oswego mill fire by George Barnard (1819-1902), later one of the most accomplished Civil War photographers, was a landmark of the daguerreotype era. It is the first known example of photojournalism. George Barnard also ran several successful daguerreotype portrait studios in Oswego and later in Syracuse, New York.

Talbot's calotype made few inroads in America, but the paper print provided an ideal artistic medium for the Scottish collaborators David Octavius Hill (1802-1870) and Robert Adamson (1821-1848) who used it for naturally posed and expressively shadowed portraits and views of Scottish architecture. Thomas Annan (1829-1887), also a versatile practitioner of Talbot's

process, later was to produce a historic volume(of forty carbon prints) documenting Glasgow's slums. In England Talbot's patent discouraged widespread use of the calotype. Gentleman painter and solicitor Roger Fenton (1819-1869), active in photographic circles as an organizer and promoter, produced artistic calotype still lifes, landscapes, portraits of the royal family, and views of Russia. But he turned to the wet-plate collodion process for his most important work – some 360 views of Crimean War battlefields.

The most impressive work of the calotype era came from France in the form of elegant landscapes, architectural views and street scenes by Gustave Le Gray, Henri Le Secq (1818-1882), Edouard-Denis Baldus (1813-1882), Charles Nègre (1820-1880), and Charles Marville (1816-1879). Maxime Du Camp (1822-1894) produced views of the ancient ruins of the Middle East in the 1850s.

Although in the collodion era (from the mid-1850s on) Marville, the first official photographer of the city of Paris, continued to do some of his most significant work using the wet-plate process, the focus in France began to shift to portraiture, with important innovations and work coming from the studios of Disdéri, Etienne Carjat (1826-1906) and Nadar (1820-1910). In 1858 Nadar, a vigorous self-promoter, made the first aerial photographs from a balloon. Photographs of exotic places remained a strong interest, and Désiré Charnay (1828-1915) surveyed the pre-Columbian ruins of Mexico and central America.

The collodion process paved the way for a golden age of travel photography in Britain. Frith's Middle East photographs; Samuel Bourne's (1834-1912) views of India, Burma and Ceylon; and Felice Beato's (c. 1830-1906) and James Robertson's (active 1852-1865) views of the Mediterranean, the Middle East, India, China and Japan explored the boundaries of the British Empire. After Scotland's John Thomson (1837-1921) produced a unique body of work on China, Hong Kong and Cambodia, he returned to expose the lives of the poor in the streets of London in the 1870s. Meanwhile, the marvels of the Industrial Revolution were revealed in the 1850s by Robert Howlett's photo essay on the construction of the steamship *Great Eastern*, and Philip Henry Dela-

motte's (1820-1889) record of the reconstruction of London's Crystal Palace at a new location.

Canadian William Notman (1826-1896) was known for portraits enhanced by elaborate wilderness settings recreated in the studio and for views of Canadian life. He established a successful chain of studios extending south to New York. Canadian-born Napoleon Sarony (1821-1896) produced over 40,000 theatrical celebrity portraits in his New York studio.

The greatest achievement of American photography of the collodion era lay in the coverage of the Civil War by such talented cameramen as Alexander Gardner (1821-1882), Timothy O'Sullivan (1840-1882), Andrew J. Russell (1830-1902) and George Barnard. With the skills they had learned and honed in their war work, Gardner, O'Sullivan and Russell went west to record the opening of the American frontier, the construction of the railroads, the natural wonders and geological eccentricities of the region, and its Native American residents. They were joined in this heroic venture by Carleton Watkins (1825-1916), John K. Hillers (1843-1925) and William Henry Jackson (1843-1942). British-

Opposite: This daguerreotype of the 1853 fire at the Ames Mill in Oswego, New York, by George Barnard, is the first known work of photojournalism.

Right: Roger Fenton's photography wagon. Using the wet collodion process, Fenton was responsible for the first systematic photographic war coverage, in Crimea in 1855.

Above: Aerial photography was all the rage after Nadar's 1858 view from a balloon. In 1860 James Wallace Black shot this aerial view of Boston, Massachusetts, entitled *Boston from the Air.*

born Eadweard Muybridge (1830-1904), who also photographed romantic western landscapes, went on to distinction with his ground-breaking studies of sequential animal and human motion, an area also investigated by American painter Thomas Eakins (1844-1916) and France's Etienne Jules Marey (1830-1904).

A new revolution came at the end of the 1880s with George Eastman's (1854-1932) introduction of the hand-held camera and celluloid-base roll film. These innovations opened up photography to amateurs on a wide scale. Masters of the artless snapshot aesthetic included France's Jacques Henri Lartrigue (1894-1988) and England's Paul Martin (1864-1942). Women, who had shied away from photography because of the heavy and cumbersome equipment, now began to engage in photography in significant numbers. While some, like Alice Austen (1866-1952) of Staten Island, concentrated on family life, others, like Frances Benjamin Johnston (1864-1952) forged successful commercial careers. Johnston went on to become the first

Above: Thomas Eakins' *Pole Vaulter (George Reynolds)*, 1884. Eakins experimented with human stop-motion photography using a technique based on one invented by French physiologist Etienne Jules Marey.

Below: An albumen print by Frederick Church of George Eastman holding a No. 2 Kodak camera on board a ship in 1880.

woman press photographer, while still finding time to delve into pictorialism.

The pictorialists sought to create soft focus, tonal, deliberately composed and often allegorical compositions resembling the paintings of Rembrandt or the French Impressionists. This style, pioneered in the 1850s in England by Oscar Rejlander (1813-1875) and Henry Peach Robinson (1830-1901) informed the work of such accomplished amateurs as Julia Margaret Cameron (1815-1879), Lewis Carroll (1832-1898) and Lady Clementina Hawarden (1822-1865). Some of the finest British pictorialism came from Peter Henry Emerson (1856-1936), Frederick H. Evans (1853-1943), Alvin Langdon Coburn (1882-1966) and Scotsman J. Craig Annan (1864-1946). In the United States pictorialism was dominated by Edward Steichen (1879-1973), Gertrude Käsebier (1852-1934), Arnold Genthe (1868-1942), F. Holland Day (1864-1933), Edward Curtis (1868-1952) and Clarence H. White (1871-1925). (White was also an influential teacher of photography).

At the same time a more realistic approach to photography was pursued by Eugène Atget (1857-1927) who exhaustively documented the architecture and streets of Paris, Brassai (1899-1984) who explored Paris night life, and photojournalist Henri Cartier-Bresson (1908-   ) who formulated the concept of the "decisive moment." Documentary photography as an instrument of social reform was pioneered in the United States by Jacob Riis (1849-1914) and Lewis Hine (1874-1940). The government-funded photographers of

Opposite top right and left: Oscar Rejlander's photographs for Charles Darwin's book, *Expressions of the Emotions* of 1873: "Sneering and Defiance" and "Fear".

Opposite: This picture taken by James R. Applegate shows the Jury of the Philadelphia Photographic Salon in 1899. Clockwise from top left: F. Holland Day, Clarence H. White, Gertrude Käsebier, Henry Troth, Frances Benjamin Johnston.

Above: From left to right, Frank Eugene, Alfred Stieglitz, Heinrich Kuehn and Edward Steichen pictured in 1907.

Right: An advertisement for Frances Benjamin Johnston's Photographic Services, circa 1896.

Depression-era America followed in their footsteps, including Dorothea Lange (1905-1965), Arthur Rothstein (1915-1987) and Walker Evans (1903-1975).

Meanwhile the influential photographer Alfred Stieglitz (1864-1946), who had previously promoted the pictorialists in his journal *Camera Work*, turned to modernism in his own work and in his vigorous promotion of the "straight photography" pursued by Paul Strand (1890-1976), Ansel Adams (1902-1984), Edward Weston (1886-1958), Imogen Cunningham (1883-1976) and others. A different modernism, which sought to parallel such art movements as Cubism, Constructivism and Surrealism was the realm of László Moholy-Nagy (1895-1946), Alexander Rodchenko (1891-1956) and Man Ray (1890-1976). Man Ray's surrealist "Rayographs" ironically were a twentieth-century reincarnation of William Henry Fox Talbot's "photogenic drawings" of the first years of photography.

VIEWS AND VISTAS

The oldest surviving photographic image, taken by Niépce around 1827 from his window, is of a humble building – a dovecote. A great number of the finest nineteenth-century photographs are of architecture because structures were an ideal subject. They were both impressive and artistic, and unlike human subjects, buildings sat still uncomplainingly for the very long exposure times required by the primitive tools and materials of photography in its infancy. Niépce's historic exposure took over eight hours to complete. Only with advances in the technology of early photography came the ability to expand the repertoire of views (a commonly used nineteenth-century term for this type of subject matter) to cityscapes, street scenes, interiors, aerial photography, panoramas, seascapes and landscapes.

Architecture had become a focus of intense interest in the nineteenth century. The rediscovery of monuments of the ancient world contributed to the redesign of equally commanding imperial cities of the modern era. At the same time an antiquarian appreciation of national styles – notably the medieval and gothic architecture of Britain and France – was fueled by the writings of such revivalists and preservationists as Pugin and Viollet-le-Duc. An understanding of architecture as a cultural relic and a political symbol inspired the 1851 photographic survey sponsored by the French Commission on Historical Monuments to inventory the nation's castles, bridges and churches with an eye toward their restoration. This project employed the considerable talents of Hippolyte Bayard, Gustave Le Gray, Edouard Baldus and Henri Le Secq. A later governmental project engaged Charles Marville to document the streets of old Paris before they were destroyed to make way for the grand boulevards. France was unique in its establishment of an official photographic archive in the nineteenth century. In the twentieth century the United States government sponsored architectural work by photographers during the Depression.

Elsewhere in the nineteenth century, in Britain and North America, architectural photography came from the cameras of independent photographers. An exception was the work of Andrew J. Russell and George Barnard. During the American Civil War, both of them worked for the Union army while on Sherman's march. In the early years of photography, ambitious daguerreotypists like John Plumbe, who photographed Washington's major federal buildings, provided views of important buildings and streets in many American cities. Some even attempted multi-plate panoramas of the urban topography of such cities as San Francisco. A more specialized form of architectural photography documented in detail the construction of important buildings, such as London's Crystal Palace or the Paris Opera.

In the domestic realm, cameramen photographed private dwellings – from the palaces of the aristocracy to the sod houses of western American settlers – enriching family memories and albums everywhere. Hence architectural photography began to provide a steady source of income from private and public commissions, as well as from the sale of mass produced photographic prints of important structures and famous sites to the public. Such views came in the form of individual prints, stereographs, numbered series, or assembled albums. As a profitable area of commercial photography, architectural photography helped to establish the careers and reputations of a number of pioneering women photographers, among them Frances Benjamin Johnston, Laura Gilpin (1891-1979), Margaret Bourke-White (1904-1971) and Berenice Abbott (1898-1991).

The style of architectural photography drew on the earlier tradition of architectural renderings or drawings. Most conservative was the classic elevation or direct head-on view. This objective approach contrasts with the expressive results achieved from a subjective treatment – the exploitation of angles, shadows, light, texture, mass, volume and close-up details to recreate for the viewer a sense of atmosphere, place and experience of the building. A viewpoint that looks up from below or looks down from above can emphasize the mass, soaring height, dynamism and urban context of the structure. The photographer can insert personal commentary or symbolic meaning by what he or she chooses to include, to either contrast or harmonize with the central structure.

Some of the most memorable views of the nineteenth century were travel photographs. While more efficient transportation, the increasing wealth of the middle class, and the consolidation of empires in Africa and Asia made such destinations accessible to more people, for others who could not travel, travel literature and photography were a way to enjoy such adventures vicariously. For easterners in the United States, western views were also a popular form of travel photography. For those who did travel, the cityscapes and landscapes were souvenirs and evidence of their journey.

ALFRED STIEGLITZ
SPRING SHOWERS, NEW YORK, n.d.
GIFT OF J. B. NEWMANN, 1958,
THE METROPOLITAN MUSEUM OF ART, NEW YORK, NY (58.577.6)

WILLIAM HENRY FOX TALBOT
STUDY OF TREES, c. 1840
THE SCIENCE MUSEUM, LONDON (1482/74)

MAXIME DU CAMP
COLOSSUS OF RAMSES II AT ABU SIMBEL, 1852
VICTORIA & ALBERT MUSEUM, LONDON

EDOUARD-DENIS BALDUS
CHALET A ENGHEIN, C. 1855
Albumen print
COURTESY GEORGE EASTMAN HOUSE, ROCHESTER, NY

CLAUDE-JOSEPH DÉSIRÉ CHARNAY
FAÇADE, GOVERNOR'S PALACE, UXMAL, 1860
Albumen print, 13¼ × 16¼ in.
COLLECTION OF J. PAUL GETTY MUSEUM, MALIBU, CA (84.XP.960.28)

EADWEARD MUYBRIDGE
FALLS OF THE YOSEMITE FROM GLACIER ROCK, 1872
Albumen print
UNIVERSITY RESEARCH LIBRARY, DEPARTMENT OF SPECIAL COLLECTIONS
UCLA, LOS ANGELES, CA

EADWEARD MUYBRIDGE
VOLCANO QUELZALTENANGO GUATEMALA, 1875
STANFORD UNIVERSITY LIBRARIES, DEPARTMENT OF SPECIAL COLLECTIONS
STANFORD, CA (RBCTR140.M97)

NOTMAN STUDIOS
ICE PALACE, DOMINION SQUARE, MONTREAL, 1884
MCCORD MUSEUM OF CANADIAN HISTORY, NOTMAN PHOTOGRAPHIC
ARCHIVES, MONTREAL

WILLIAM HENRY JACKSON
OUTSIDE THE WALL AT PEKING, 1895
LIBRARY OF CONGRESS, WASHINGTON, DC

FREDERICK H. EVANS
A SEA OF STEPS, WELLS CATHEDRAL, 1903
Gelatin silver print
COURTESY GEORGE EASTMAN HOUSE, ROCHESTER, NY

Eugène Atget
Boulevard de Strasbourg, Corsets, 1912
COLLECTION OF BERENICE ABBOTT

LÁSZLÓ MOHOLY-NAGY
ROTHENBURG, 1925-1930
Gelatin silver print, 9⅙ × 6¹³⁄₁₆ in.
COLLECTION OF J. PAUL GETTY MUSEUM, MALIBU, CA (84.XP.124.1)

LAURA GILPIN
TAOS OVENS, NEW MEXICO, 1926
Platinum print
LIBRARY OF CONGRESS, WASHINGTON, DC

ANSEL ADAMS
SAGUAROS, n.d.
NATIONAL ARCHIVES

BERENICE ABBOTT
BREAD STORE, FEBRUARY 3, 1937
FEDERAL ARTS PROJECT "CHANGING NEW YORK"
MUSEUM OF THE CITY OF NEW YORK, NY (#199)

ARTISTRY AND EXPRESSION

Whether photography could express artistry as well as it could record reality was an issue from its very beginnings. The subjects, compositions and themes of painting, sculpture and engraving informed the work of many photographers throughout the nineteenth century and well into the twentieth. The major divisions of the traditional visual arts – portraiture, landscape, genre, history and still life – all found a place in photography. The pioneers of photography found still life to be an ideal subject. For Niépce, a table top displaying dishes and food; for Daguerre, a collection of shells; and for Bayard, an arrangement of plaster casts of antique sculptures, were all subjects that were well-suited to the long exposure times necessary in early photography. Later, more artfully arranged still lifes by Fenton, Le Secq and others extended a tradition practiced in baroque painting. The studio portrait photographers who provided elegant settings of swagged drapery, Greek columns, oriental carpets and decorative urns – elements suggesting social status and wealth – were also employing a well-known convention of portrait painting in the grand style.

The nineteenth-century European and American world view was largely sentimental and symbolic. In many cases, therefore, the landscapes and architectural views of ambitious photographers were more than just beautiful pictures reminiscent of paintings by the old masters. Foreign views could reflect imperial power and economic possession; ancient ruins could relate moral tales about the folly of hubris; and stalwart old buildings could be regarded as visible symbols of enduring national culture and historic patrimony. The classically balanced and harmonious pastoral landscape – an expression of the picturesque aesthetic – could evoke nostalgic meditations on a primeval paradise. Other more dynamic landscapes, with soaring peaks, jagged precipices and stormy skies – expressions of the sublime – could provoke awe and suggest God's instrumentality.

An inherent artistry arose from the materials and processes of photography. The calotype, Talbot's image on paper, considered inferior by some because of its lack of detail when compared with the daguerreotype, could appear painterly in the hands of the right photographer. The expressive calotypes of Scotland's Hill and Adamson were to inspire the later pictorialists or art photographers. Pictorialism arose from the "high art" movement started by England's Oscar Rejlander with his controversial *The Two Ways of Life* (based on Raphael's *The School of Athens*), an elaborate combination print assembled from numerous negatives. Henry Peach Robinson used Rejlander's assemblage procedure to create moral allegories and sentimental narrative tableaux peopled with costumed "actors." Following Rejlander and Robinson came the less stilted efforts of Lewis Carroll and Julia Margaret Cameron, whose portraits and costume pieces illustrating mythological, religious and literary themes were inspired by the pre-Raphaelite painters. Rejecting such artifice, Peter Henry Emerson urged a more purist approach focusing on scenes from nature.

In the 1890s a new form of pictorialism based on Impressionist painting and the work of the Dutch masters, began to utilize soft-focus tonal and atmospheric effects achieved through manipulations in the developing and printing processes. In the United States, Alfred Stieglitz, in a deliberate attempt to raise photography to the level of the other fine arts, featured the work of Gertrude Käsebier, F. Holland Day, Edward Steichen, Clarence H. White and others, along with that of British pictorialists Frederick Evans and J. Craig Annan, in the journals *Camera Notes* and *Camera Work*, and in a series of exhibitions.

A revolt against the self-conscious artiness of the pictorialists came with the "straight photography" practiced by Paul Strand, Ansel Adams, Imogen Cunningham, Edward Weston and other members of California's f/64 Group. Such avant-garde art movements as Cubism, Vorticism, Constructivism and Surrealism inspired still other modernist photographers, including Man Ray, László Moholy-Nagy, Alvin Langdon Coburn, Francis Bruguière (1879-1945), André Kertész (1894-1987) and Alexander Rodchenko. With his abstract cloud images which he called equivalents, Alfred Stieglitz created a photographic abstract expressionism.

The first decades of the twentieth century also saw the rise of advertising and fashion photography, often executed by fine art photographers such as Man Ray or Edward Steichen. A number of photographers came to specialize in fashion work, among them Adolph De Meyer (1886-1946), Horst P. Horst (1906-   ), George Platt Lynes (1907-1955) and Martin Munkacsi (1896-1963). American Toni Frissell (1907-   ) helped to forge a less mannered version of fashion photography based on the snapshot aesthetic. The finest art and fashion photographers both relied less on literal translation than on expressive reinterpretation of contemporaneous art styles.

GERTRUDE KÄSEBIER
FRENCH LANDSCAPE, c. 1900
LIBRARY OF CONGRESS, WASHINGTON, DC

HENRI LE SECQ
STILL LIFE, FANTASIE PHOTOGRAPHIQUE
Gelatin silver print
COURTESY GEORGE EASTMAN HOUSE, ROCHESTER, NY

HENRY PEACH ROBINSON
THE LADY OF SHALOTT, 1861
Albumen print
ROYAL PHOTOGRAPHIC SOCIETY, BATH, ENGLAND

PETER HENRY EMERSON
A POND IN WINTER
Platinum print
COURTESY GEORGE EASTMAN HOUSE, ROCHESTER, NY

CLEMENTINA HAWARDEN
YOUNG GIRL WITH MIRROR REFLECTION, 1860s
Albumen print
VICTORIA & ALBERT MUSEUM, LONDON

EDWARD CURTIS
THE VANISHING RACE – NAVAHO
LIBRARY OF CONGRESS, WASHINGTON, DC

CARLETON WATKINS
MIRROR LAKE, YOSEMITE, No. 75, 1878
*RARE BOOK DEPT., HISTORICAL PHOTOGRAPHS, THE HUNTINGTON LIBRARY,
SAN MARINO, CA*

CLARENCE H. WHITE
RING TOSS, 1899
Platinum print
LIBRARY OF CONGRESS, WASHINGTON, DC

GERTRUDE KÄSEBIER
"BLESSED ART THOU AMONG WOMEN", c. 1899
LIBRARY OF CONGRESS, WASHINGTON, DC

ALFRED STIEGLITZ & CLARENCE H. WHITE
TORSO, 1907
LIBRARY OF CONGRESS, WASHINGTON, DC

F. HOLLAND DAY
PRODIGAL'S RETURN, 1909
LIBRARY OF CONGRESS, WASHINGTON, DC

LAURA GILPIN
THE PRELUDE, 1917
Platinum print
LIBRARY OF CONGRESS, WASHINGTON, DC

ALVIN LANGDON COBURN
VORTOGRAPH (abstract photograph from reflecting mirrors), 1917
Silver gelatin print
HAROLD L. STUART ENDOWMENT, © 1995,
THE ART INSTITUTE OF CHICAGO, IL. ALL RIGHTS RESERVED (1987.379)

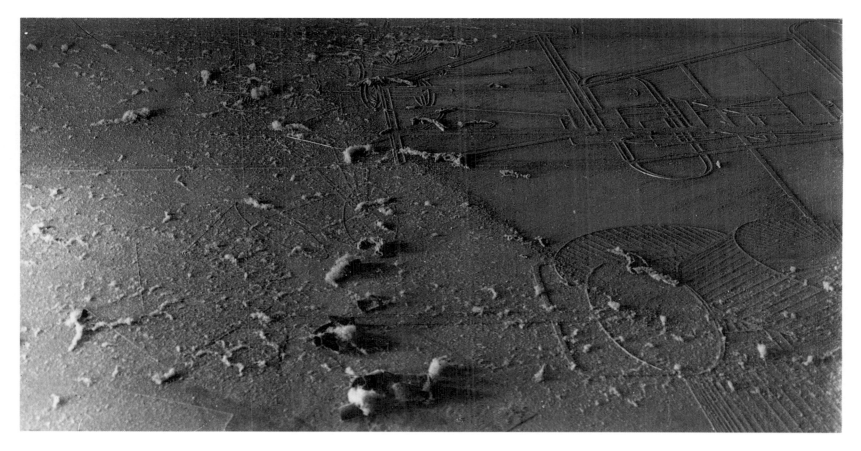

MAN RAY
DUST BREEDING, 1920
Gelatin silver print, 8¼ × 16 in.
PURCHASE WITH FUNDS FROM GEORGIA PACIFIC CORP.
HIGH MUSEUM OF ART, ATLANTA, GA (1984.223)

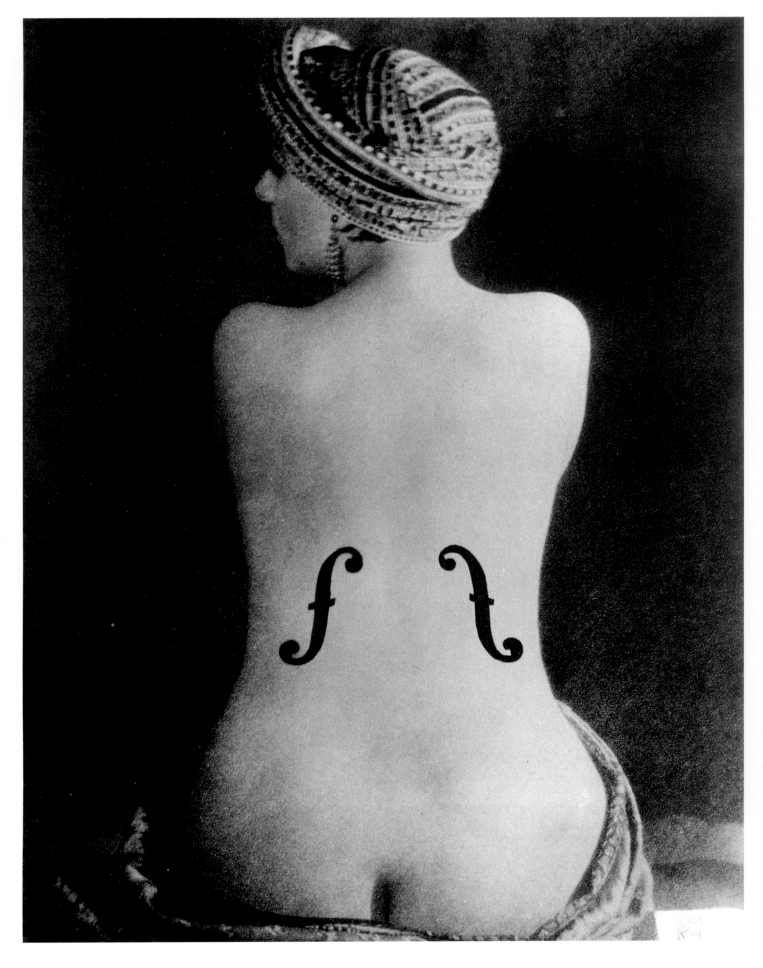

MAN RAY
LE VIOLIN D'INGRES (INGRES' VIOLIN), 1924
Gelatin silver print, 11⅝ × 9 in.
COLLECTION OF THE J. PAUL GETTY MUSEUM, MALIBU, CA (86.XM.626.10)

IMOGEN CUNNINGHAM
MAGNOLIA BLOSSOM, 1925
Gelatin silver print, 9³⁄₁₅ × 11⅝ in.
HENRY SWIFT COLLECTION, GIFT OF FLORENCE ALSTON SWIFT,
SAN FRANCISCO MUSEUM OF MODERN ART, SAN FRANCISCO, CA (62.19.112)

Francis Bruguière
Double Portrait, c. 1925
Solarized gelatin silver print
COURTESY GEORGE EASTMAN HOUSE, ROCHESTER, NY

ANDRÉ KERTÉSZ
CHEZ MONDRIAN, 1926
VICTORIA & ALBERT MUSEUM, LONDON

EDWARD WESTON
TWO SHELLS, 1927
Gelatin silver print, 9⁹⁄₁₆ × 7 in.
ALBERT M. BENDER COLLECTION, BEQUEST OF ALBERT M. BENDER
SAN FRANCISCO MUSEUM OF MODERN ART, SAN FRANCISCO, CA (41.2995)

LÁSZLÓ MOHOLY-NAGY
BERLIN RADIO TOWER, c. 1928
Gelatin silver print, 14⁷⁄₁₆ × 10⁷⁄₈ in.
JULIEN LEVY COLLECTION, SPECIAL PHOTOGRAPHY ACQUISITION FUND
© *1995, THE ART INSTITUTE OF CHICAGO, IL, ALL RIGHTS RESERVED (1979.84)*

LÁSZLÓ MOHOLY-NAGY
UNTITLED (ABSTRACTION), n.d.
Gelatin silver print, 20 × 16 in.
GIFT OF GEORGE AND RUTH BARFORD, © 1995, THE ART INSTITUTE OF
CHICAGO, IL, ALL RIGHTS RESERVED (1968.264)

ARNOLD GENTHE
MARIAN MORGAN GROUP (II), c. 1930
LIBRARY OF CONGRESS, WASHINGTON, DC

FACES AND FIGURES

When the invention of the daguerreotype was announced in 1839, many foresaw portraiture as its most practical and profitable application. At the time, the primitive state of daguerreotype technology made this an impossibility – initially a subject would have had to spend a quarter of an hour in frozen rigidity under the full sun in order to obtain an acceptable result. But the sitting time, assisted by a clamp behind the head, was soon reduced to less than a minute, thanks to rapid improvements in the process and materials of the daguerreotype.

Photography began to challenge the supremacy of portrait painting both in realism of depiction and in cost. A miniature painting by a competent itinerant artist cost around $15, while a daguerreotype cost from $10 to as little as 25¢, depending on its size and whether it was taken by a noted studio photographer or by an itinerant cameraman. Yet while daguerreotypy was hailed for its democratizing influence, by bringing portraiture to the masses, it was also regarded with ambivalence. A daguerreotype rendered a realistic image of the sitter and so could be pitiless in its revelation of homeliness, while a portrait painter could easily improve on a sitter's less attractive features. A sensitive and artistic photographer, however, could also create a desirable image with a careful choice of pose, dress, hair arrangement, background, accessories, and light and shadow. Albert Southworth, one of the finest daguerreotype portraitists, noted,

> Nature is not at all to be represented as it is, but as it ought to be, and might possibly have been; and it is required of, and should be the aim of, the artist-photographer to produce in the likeness the best possible character and finest expression of which that particular face or figure could ever have been capable. . . .

In the nineteenth century, character rather than beauty was the attribute held in the highest esteem, and it was this that a photographer strove to capture. The type and nature of superficial facial and cranial features, as delineated by the pseudo-sciences of physiognomy and phrenology, provided essential clues to the true moral character of a person. This interpretation of portraiture underlay the creation in the United States of a pantheon of photographs of leading citizens whose faces, as a group, symbolized the American character. First Edward Anthony and John Plumbe, and then Mathew Brady assiduously photographed members of the nation's political, intellectual and artistic elite, initially in exchange for a free portrait and later for a sitting fee. The studio operators displayed these images in galleries and the public came to study the famous faces, to draw moral lessons from them, and to have their own portraits taken.

The exploitation of famous faces for entertainment and commercial ends flourished in the subsequent collodion era which saw the mass production of millions of cartes-de-visite. Very low in cost, these miniature celebrity portraits could now be purchased by the public, collected into albums and studied at leisure in one's own parlor. Originating in France with André-Adolphe Eugène Disdéri's innovations, the celebrity carte-de-visite became an important source of revenue for the versatile Nadar who photographed his bohemian circle of Parisian writers and artists. In the United States, Napoleon Sarony excelled in portraying the theatrical stars of the day in unusual settings and poses, often created in collaboration with the subject.

Accomplished amateurs like Lewis Carroll and Julia Margaret Cameron photographed their circle of family and friends, often in allegorical costumes and poses suggested by and resembling paintings. Photographers who made self-portraits sometimes used them as occasions to experiment with unorthodox poses and settings. The pictorialists of the turn of the century produced atmospheric soft-focus portraits using texture, light and shadow for artistic expressiveness. Edward Curtis subordinated individuality in his pictorialist catalogue of Native Americans as symbolic representations of a type – the noble red man. While claiming ethnological correctness of detail, he sometimes costumed his sitters in more exotic or "typical" apparel. Alfred Stieglitz conceived the idea of the composite portrait – ideally a lifelong documentation of an individual, as a whole and in visual fragments, in varying moods, attitudes and roles – which he attempted with Georgia O'Keeffe. Modernist ideas and motifs from Cubism and Surrealism inspired innovative portraits by Rodchenko, Man Ray and others, as well as the work of fashion photographers.

Documentarians, who customarily surveyed the underclass rather than the elite of society, produced a range of powerful images. E. J. Bellocq's (1873-1949) women in a New Orleans brothel, Brassai's Parisians at night, Doris Ulmann's (1882-1934) rural poor of Appalachia, and August Sander's (1876-1964) German citizens classified by social type and occupation for his monumental project "Man in the Twentieth Century", all emerge with a directness and dignity uncompromised by artistic manipulations.

LOTTE JACOBI
HEAD OF A DANCER, c. 1929
Gelatin silver print, 16⁷/₁₆ × 6¹⁵/₁₆ in.
PURCHASE WITH EXCHANGE FUNDS FROM THE EDWARD JOSEPH GALLAGHER III
MEMORIAL COLLECTION, AND PARTIAL GIFT OF GEORGE DALSHEIMER, BALTIMORE
THE BALTIMORE MUSEUM OF ART, BALTIMORE, MD (BMA-1988.368)

ALBERT SOUTHWORTH & JOSIAH HAWES
UNKNOWN LADY, n.d.
Daguerreotype, 8½ × 6½ in.
GIFT OF EDWARD SOUTHWORTH HAWES IN MEMORY OF HIS FATHER, JOSIAH
JOHNSON HAWES, COURTESY, MUSEUM OF FINE ARTS, BOSTON, MA (43.1405)

ROBERT HOWLETT
PORTRAIT OF ISAMBARD KINGDOM BRUNEL AND LAUNCHING CHAINS
OF THE GREAT EASTERN, 1857
Albumen print from wet collodion negative, 15¹⁵/₁₆ × 8¹³/₁₆ in.
VICTORIA & ALBERT MUSEUM, LONDON

Nadar
Sarah Bernhardt, 1859
Gelatin silver print
COURTESY GEORGE EASTMAN HOUSE, ROCHESTER, NY

ANDRÉ ADOLPHE EUGÈNE DISDÉRI
PRINCESS BONAPARTE GABRIELLI
Uncut carte-de-visite
*GERNSHEIM COLLECTION, HARRY RANSOM HUMANITIES RESEARCH CENTER,
THE UNIVERSITY OF TEXAS AT AUSTIN, TX*

JULIA MARGARET CAMERON
SIR JOHN HERSCHEL, 1867
Albumen print, 13 × 10⅙ in.
A GIFT OF MRS. J. D. CAMERON BRADLEY
COURTESY, MUSEUM OF FINE ARTS, BOSTON, MA (42.328)

LEWIS CARROLL
ALICE LIDDELL AS A BEGGAR MAID
MORRIS L. PARRISH COLLECTION, DEPARTMENT OF RARE BOOKS
AND SPECIAL COLLECTIONS,
PRINCETON UNIVERSITY LIBRARIES, PRINCETON, NJ

ALICE AUSTEN
FULL LENGTH WITH FAN ON AUSTEN PIAZZA, 1892
EAA COLLECTION, COURTESY OF THE STATEN ISLAND HISTORICAL SOCIETY,
STATEN ISLAND, NY

ALVIN LANGDON COBURN
GEORGE BERNARD SHAW, 1905
LIBRARY OF CONGRESS, WASHINGTON, DC

EDWARD STEICHEN
J. P. MORGAN, c. 1903
THE ALFRED STIEGLITZ COLLECTION,
THE METROPOLITAN MUSEUM OF ART, NEW YORK, NY (49.55.167)

EDWARD CURTIS
PLACATING THE SPIRIT OF A SLAIN EAGLE – ASSINIBOIN
LIBRARY OF CONGRESS, WASHINGTON, DC

ALEXANDER RODCHENKO
CRITIC OSIP BRIK (KRITIK OSIP BRIK), 1924
Gelatin silver print, 11¼ × 8³⁄₁₆ in.
COLLECTION OF THE J. PAUL GETTY MUSEUM, MALIBU, CA (84.XM.258.30)

ADOLF DE MEYER
PORTRAIT OF JOSEPHINE BAKER, 1925
Gelatin silver print, 15⅜ × 15⅝ in.
COLLECTION OF THE J. PAUL GETTY MUSEUM, MALIBU, CA (84.XP.960.28)

ARNOLD GENTHE
GRETA GARBO, 1925
LIBRARY OF CONGRESS, WASHINGTON, DC

DORIS ULMANN
WILLIAM CAMPBELL, ABINGTON, VA, circa 1930
LIBRARY OF CONGRESS, WASHINGTON, DC

BRASSAÏ
BIJOU OF MONTMARTRE, c. 1933
VICTORIA & ALBERT MUSEUM, LONDON

AUGUST SANDER
YOUNG SOLDIER, WESTERWALD, 1945
Gelatin silver print, 11¹¹/₁₆ × 9⅛ in.
MR. AND MRS. HARRISON R. JOHNSON, JR. FUND
THE MINNEAPOLIS INSTITUTE OF THE ARTS, MINNEAPOLIS, MN (77.68.1)
© AUGUST SANDER ARCHIV/KULTURSTIFTUNG STADTSPARKASSE KÖLN;
VG BILD-KUNST, BONN 1995

DOCUMENTATION

Photography's most powerful attribute is its ability to reproduce reality accurately. Ideally the documentary photographer is an objective eyewitness to unmanipulated events or subjects. Hence, early on, photography was found by scientists to be the perfect tool for preserving their observations of the world around them. The camera was used to record the phases of the moon, the physiology of criminals and the insane, the clouds in the sky, the wounds of Civil War soldiers, and the sequential movement of humans and animals in the projects of Eadweard Muybridge.

With the opening of the American frontier, photographers Timothy O'Sullivan and William Henry Jackson were hired as key members of the government expeditions of the 1860s and 1870s to the West. Details of the flora, fauna and distinctive geological features of the region were captured laboriously on wet-plate glass negatives. A remarkable series of views of the Yellowstone area was assembled into albums for presentation to federal officials, thus influencing them to preserve Yellowstone as the country's first national park.

Art history and the social sciences also benefited from the documentary lens. The French government commissioned Hippolyte Bayard, Gustave Le Gray, Edouard Baldus and Charles Marville to record for posterity the historic buildings of the nation and the streets of old Paris. Charles Nègre documented working class people on the streets and as patients in the Vincennes Imperial Asylum. Around the turn of the century Eugène Atget began his extensive inventory of the architecture, shop windows and occupational types of Paris before the modern age changed everything. The lives of upper middle class French and their fascination with new inventions were captured by Jacques Henri Lartigue, who photographed his own family circle.

In the American West, Solomon D. Butcher's (1958-1927) photographs preserved the worn faces of pioneers posing in front of their primitive sod houses, while the ceremonies and adobe dwellings of the Native Americans of the Southwest were recorded in photographs by John K. Hillers, Edward Curtis and others. In the Far East, Scotsman John Thomson completed a detailed series on the lives of the Chinese before returning to document the poor of London for the landmark book, *Street Life in London*. Decades later, using a concealed camera, Arnold Genthe photographed the street life of San Francisco's Chinatown.

Documentary photography became an agent of social reform in the hands of muckraking American journalist Jacob Riis, who raised awareness about the deplorable living conditions of immigrants on New York's Lower East Side and helped to bring about reforms in housing, education and working conditions. Lewis Hine continued this reform movement by documenting children working in mines and factories. His projects include a record of living conditions in the war-ravaged Europe of 1918, a 1926 series on immigrants arriving at Ellis Island, and the construction of the Empire State Building in 1930. Achievements of industry were recorded by Edward Weston, Margaret Bourke-White and Charles Sheeler (1883-1965).

During the Depression, the Farm Security Administration, a United States government agency, sent photographers out to document the problems affecting the rural poor. At work on this project were Dorothea Lange, Arthur Rothstein, Walker Evans and others who produced powerful and moving images from the nation's heartland. The Works Project Administration kept Berenice Abbott at work on *Changing New York*, a systematic documentation of all facets of the metropolitan environment. In doing so, Abbott followed in the footsteps of Atget whom she had befriended in Paris and whose work she had saved.

Some of the most enduring images of documentary photography come from photojournalism, the recording of newsworthy events. While some early images, such as Southworth and Hawes's daguerreotype of a surgical operation had to be restaged for the camera, George Barnard's 1853 view of the Oswego mill fire was the genuine article. The finest achievement of nineteenth-century photojournalism was the coverage of the American Civil War. Although Roger Fenton had pioneered war photography with his series on the Crimean War, the Civil War coverage was unprecedented in its scope, depth and sheer numbers of cameramen at work, including Mathew Brady's teams, Alexander Gardner, Andrew J. Russell, Timothy O'Sullivan and Barnard.

The development of the halftone process in the 1890s made press photography possible. Frances Benjamin Johnston was the first woman to enter this career. Her other projects included portraits of official Washington, a noted series on the Hampton Institute, and a survey of the historic buildings and gardens of the American South. Henri Cartier-Bresson became one of the world's leading photojournalists with his aesthetic of the "decisive moment" – capturing the revelatory instant when all elements of a scene fall into place.

JACOB RIIS
BANDITS' ROOST, 39½ MULBERRY STREET, c. 1889
THE JACOB A. RIIS COLLECTION #101, MUSEUM OF THE CITY OF NEW YORK, NY

ROGER FENTON
CAMP OF THE FIFTH DRAGOON GUARDS,
LOOKING TOWARDS KADIKOI, 1855
LIBRARY OF CONGRESS, WASHINGTON, DC

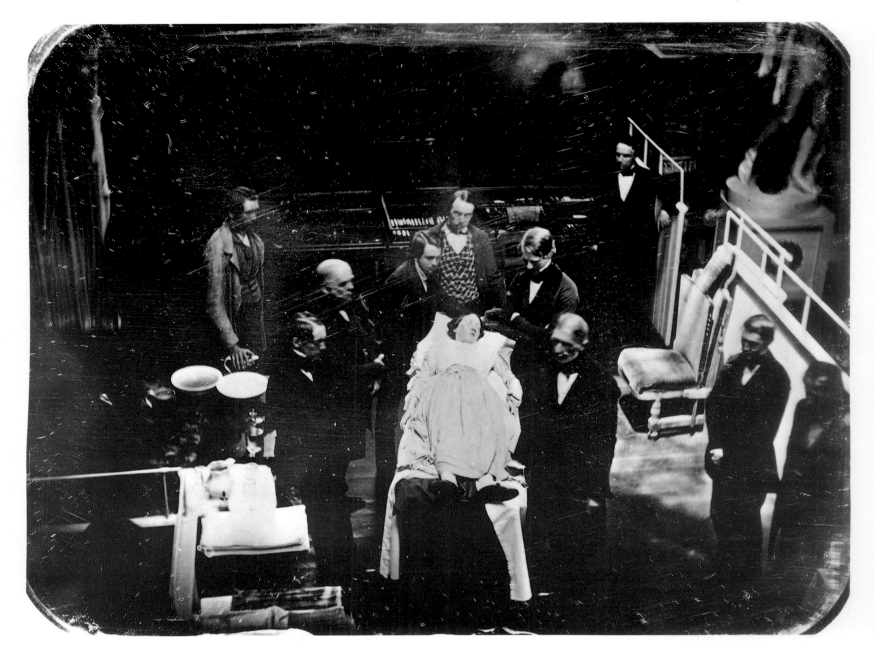

ALBERT SOUTHWORTH & JOSIAH HAWES
OPERATION UNDER ETHER AT MASSACHUSETTS GENERAL HOSPITAL,
c. 1846-47
Daguerreotype
COURTESY OF MASSACHUSETTS GENERAL HOSPITAL, BOSTON, MA

Timothy O'Sullivan
General Grant and Staff at Massaponax Church,
May 21, 1864
Library of Congress, Washington, DC

MATHEW BRADY COLLECTION
COMPANY KITCHEN, CAMP OF THE 6TH NEW YORK ARTILLERY AT
BRANDY STATION, VA, APRIL 1864
LIBRARY OF CONGRESS, WASHINGTON, DC

ANDREW J. RUSSELL
UNION SOLDIERS ENTRENCHED ALONG THE WEST BANK OF THE
RAPPAHANNOCK RIVER AT FREDERICKSBURG, MAY, 1863
NATIONAL ARCHIVES

GEORGE BARNARD
CITY OF ATLANTA, 1864
NATIONAL ARCHIVES

ALEXANDER GARDNER
THE EXECUTION OF FOUR OF THE LINCOLN CONSPIRATORS,
THE OLD PENITENTIARY, WASHINGTON, DC, July 7, 1865
THE BETTMANN ARCHIVE, NEW YORK, NY

EDWARD & HENRY T. ANTHONY
BROADWAY – FROZEN RUINS OF BARNUM'S AMERICAN MUSEUM
AS IT APPEARED IMMEDIATELY AFTER FIRE OF MARCH 3, 1868
Stereograph
COLLECTION OF THE NEW YORK HISTORICAL SOCIETY, NEW YORK, NY (502.17)

WILLIAM HENRY JACKSON
MAMMOTH HOT SPRINGS, YELLOWSTONE, 1872
PHOTO ARCHIVES, MUSEUM OF NEW MEXICO, SANTA FE, NM

TIMOTHY O'SULLIVAN
ANCIENT RUINS IN THE CANYON DE CHELLY, NEW MEXICO
(TERRITORY), 1873
PHOTO ARCHIVES, MUSEUM OF NEW MEXICO, SANTA FE, NM

JOHN THOMSON
COVENT GARDEN LABORERS, 1877-78
Woodburytype, 4⁹/₁₆ × 3⁷/₁₆ in.
VICTORIA & ALBERT MUSEUM, LONDON

SOLOMON D. BUTCHER
SYLVESTER RAWDING HOUSE, NORTH OF SARGENT, CUSTER
COUNTY, NEBRASKA, 1886
SOLOMON D. BUTCHER COLLECTION
NEBRASKA STATE HISTORICAL SOCIETY, LINCOLN, NE

WILLIAM HENRY JACKSON
GOLDI ALONG THE AMUR RIVER, 1896
LIBRARY OF CONGRESS, WASHINGTON, DC

EADWEARD MUYBRIDGE
ANIMAL LOCOMOTION PLATE 187, 1887
Collotype, 7⅛ × 16⁹⁄₁₆ in.
THE MINNEAPOLIS INSTITUTE OF THE ARTS, MINNEAPOLIS, MN (81.76.25)

FRANCES BENJAMIN JOHNSTON
"CARPENTRY CLASS," HAMPTON ALBUM, 1899-1900
LIBRARY OF CONGRESS, WASHINGTON, DC

LEWIS W. HINE
CAROLINA COTTON MILL, 1908
Gelatin silver print
COURTESY GEORGE EASTMAN HOUSE, ROCHESTER, NY

JOHN T. DANIELS
ORVILLE WRIGHT TAKING OFF, DECEMBER 17, 1903
LIBRARY OF CONGRESS, WASHINGTON, DC

ARNOLD GENTHE
THE BUTCHER, OLD CHINA TOWN, SAN FRANCISCO
LIBRARY OF CONGRESS, WASHINGTON, DC

MARGARET BOURKE-WHITE
UNTITLED (INTERIOR OF FOUNDRY), 1927-1929
Gelatin silver photograph, $12\frac{7}{8} \times 9\frac{1}{4}$ in.
MUSEUM PURCHASE WITH FUNDS PROVIDED BY THE MUNDY COMPANIES
THE MUSEUM OF FINE ARTS, HOUSTON, TX (86.348)

HENRI CARTIER-BRESSON
GARE SAINT-LAZARE, PARIS, 1932
Silver gelatin print 15¾ × 11⅞ in.
THE MENIL COLLECTION, HOUSTON, TX (FO74-06.007MF)

BERENICE ABBOTT
COURT OF THE FIRST MODEL TENEMENT
IN NEW YORK CITY, MARCH, 16, 1936
FEDERAL ARTS PROJECT "CHANGING NEW YORK,"
MUSEUM OF THE CITY OF NEW YORK, NY (#76)

LENI RIEFENSTAHL
SWIMMER, 1936 OLYMPICS
LIBRARY OF CONGRESS, WASHINGTON, DC

WALKER EVANS
ROADSIDE STAND, VICINITY OF BIRMINGHAM, AL, 1936
LIBRARY OF CONGRESS, WASHINGTON, DC

ARTHUR ROTHSTEIN
EVICTED SHARECROPPERS ALONG HIGHWAY #60, NEW MADRID
COUNTY, MO, JANUARY, 1939
LIBRARY OF CONGRESS, WASHINGTON, DC

LIST OF PHOTOGRAPHS

PHOTO CREDITS

Archives of American Art, Washington, DC: 21(top)
Bayerisches Nationalmuseum, Berlin: 10
The Bettmann Archive, New York, NY: 6, 12, 13(top)
Courtesy of the Boston Public Library, Print Department, Boston, MA: 18
From *Expression of the Emotions*, 1873, by Charles Darwin: 20(top right), 21(bottom)
Courtesy George Eastman House, Rochester, NY: 7(bottom), 8, 9(bottom), 16, 19(bottom)
Harvard College Observatory, Cambridge, MA (7908-36A): 14

Library of Congress, Washington, DC: 15, 17, 20(top left), 20(bottom right)
Metropolitan Museum of Art, Gift of Charles Bregler, New York, NY: 19(top)
National Archives: 13(bottom)
The Science Museum, London: 7(top), 9(top), 11

ACKNOWLEDGMENTS
The author and publisher of this book would like to thank the following people who helped in the preparation of this book: Sara Dunphy, the photo editor; Ron Callow of Design 23, the designer; and Margaret Gill Sobel, the editor.